Life Without Speaking

Life Without Speaking

MARY RUEFLE

The University of Alabama Press
Tuscaloosa and London

ABB-5144

PS
3568
.U36
L5
1987

11/1987
AmSi

Copyright © 1987 by
The University of Alabama Press
Tuscaloosa, Alabama 35487
All rights reserved
Manufactured in the United States of America

For Paul Valéry's quote:
Paul Valéry, *The Collected Works in English,* Bollingen Series XLV, Vol. 2: *Poems in the Rough,* trans. Hilary Corke. Copyright © 1969 by Princeton University Press.
For "The Tomb in Ghent":
This poem first appeared in *Chelsea 40* in 1981.
For "Reasons of His Own":
Reprinted by permission from *New England Review,* Vol. IV, No. 3 (1982). Copyright © 1982 by Mary Ruefle.

Library of Congress Cataloging-in-Publication Data

Ruefle, Mary, 1952–
   Life without speaking.

   (Alabama poetry series)
   I. Title. II. Series.
PS3568.U36L5 1987   811'.54   86-30717
ISBN 0-8173-0345-6
ISBN 0-8173-0346-4 (pbk.)

British Library Cataloguing-in-Publication Data is available.

For S. F.

ACKNOWLEDGMENTS

Some of these poems first appeared in the following magazines:

Black Warrior Review: "The Wife of Mission Rock," "As Many As Nine," "Stamina," "Dead Silence on a Beautiful Day," "Who Shall Have This," "Almost As If To Tell Me," "More Nights," "Lady Throwing Crackers to the Sea"
Chelsea: "The Tomb in Ghent"
Chiaroscuro: "In the Process of Elimination," "Her Rival," "Twin Trees," "Gigantic Brazen Head," "Tell Her"
Cutbank: "At Cana"
8½ × 11: "The Compulsion to Adoration"
Ironwood: "Tongues," "Patient Without an Acre"
The Missouri Review: "True to Life Also," "The Least Sequence of Flesh"
New England Review: "Reasons of His Own"
The Ohio Review: "This Untouched Thing," "How History Begins"
Porch: "Barbarians"
Sands: "The Intended," "The Inspector of Miracles," "An Examination of Suffering," "The House of His Own Undoing"

Contents

III

I know (he said), by a method of calculation previously quite unknown—I know, to within a few dozens, the number of words that I shall have spoken between my first babblings and my dying discourse.

Every word I speak therefore, I grudge it, as an irrecoverable expense.

In no way can one evade the fact that this number is finite, say N. If n is the number of words already *lost*, then N minus n remain to me.

—Paul Valéry, *Broken Stories*

I

Barbarians

Here and there, between trees,

cows lie down in the forest

in the mid-afternoon

as though sleep were an idea

for which they were willing

to die.

More Nights

The marquise says there are those
who have spent more nights than
days in this world. Some say
that is the cause of their condition.
The truth is, they belong to their
condition:
in a narrow street they pass
without thinking. Each one,
heavier than his body, carries
a badge like the one, almost
shapeless eye of March.
Secretly organized, none of the
members know each other.
There's nothing to recognize
but the terror of it,
that in death there remains
someone else for you to know.

Living Through May

Woke early without dreams,
beautiful weather and no mail.
Thought it rich to die
just once, while opening nutshells
over a pond.
The buds are out without opening.
Some say between budding
is the best time for something.
I don't know what.
I've forgotten what a thousand bees
among maple buds are murmuring about.
There's the sound of someone
gutting a fish!
It's fine with us all
that not one life
has been inspected
since dawn.

Starting to Brood

This starting to brood
again: impossible repulsive
jack-in-the-pulpit, what can
I say? The uselessness of
letters and past lives . . .
a gust of duress lengthwise
in an old book.
For ten years and ten days
nothing has happened
but a brief windstorm.
A tree in the courtyard
blown down to the ground
turned into a peacock
and flew off.
Trust your life to a single hair.
Threads end in high windy places
if you with your wits
keep fanning them from below.

Geisha Song

Peach petal wetted by rain is
incomparable, but after
twenty-five miles an hour in
second gear up Buckhill
the device of my car
slowly and very slowly
satisfies my desire
to see the peonies, showy now,
at the end of my
slippery drive.

This Untouched Thing

Sunfall:
blue barn on
glare ice,
slow-poke
to the salt lick.
One moment
intimidates the next.
You've never gone
so astray.
And the birds!
One cherry red
infiltrating the sky
like a vial of vinegars.
Nature has never been
more absent,
her whole head facing
an opposite direction
with the mentality of conifers
still standing erect.
She's whipped
to the membrane,
skin loose enough
to slip off,
suggesting an
imaginary bondage.

Turin: Red Clouds in Winter

The grande dame
of scarlets
just now loosening her powder
inside an olive jar
with a lid that keeps
turning forever . . .

and the endless unfolding
of functions,
one right inside another
like the industrious heart
of a bumblebee
huffing and puffing up stalks . . .

and the factory fumes,
their slow-rising smoke,
as if someone were finished
and exhaled in a moment
of rest . . .

Possibly for the Day After This

I spent today
lying down
in a boxwood copse,
out of the wind's reach
as it made for the trees,
watching the far tops
bow down:
it was the wind did this
like a train over violets
only it took more sound
and a greater effort:
no one living can enjoy
the wind, the trees,
the traveling life
of a boxwood copse
on a train
covered with violets.

Dead Silence on a Beautiful Day

The trees have ears like elephants
and no sense of language.
The cow with a star on her face
and a ring in her ear
didn't move. The slightest juices
thickening in the bellies of birds
were missing:
usually a moment of song
will lap at the edge of anything,
licking a rounded-out trace of itself,
but somehow a cow tongue
got lost in the mouth,
feeling its way back home.
I broke apart a round of yellow cheese
and the sound of it caused me to stop.
We've been starting and stopping
like signals shot through a porthole
and it looks like
nothing can stop the flow.
It might be the message
we've been waiting for,
the one we've been trying to send:
that phone call of light
coming through to a life
clear across water
where noise puts itself
to sleep in our hands.

Attic

So the mouse may be Buddha:
no reason to ruin his teeth
in order to show me he's able
to bite down the bone-hard teeth
of a comb that belonged to my mother
and her mother before her
and hers before that.

From Memory

The old poet riding on horseback in winter
came face to face with a thief who had
beaten his horse to a pulp. Once and for
all, they recognized each other without
speaking; one held a bright knife to the
other's throat while the other offered the
bleeding velvet of his animal to show that
he, too, had smuggled his life through
every conceivable hour.

Aubade

for Dara Wier

My elbows are wet
and my fingers cold
from washing the lovely
white slip you sent.
It fits between the pews
of an apple orchard,
drying on the hands
of a little tree
wearing white socks.
It's got the whole church
standing akimbo,
ironing out violets
like spots from a nosebleed.
There'll be no more snow.
A black note falls on the
keyboard, and discovers
its sins are missing!

Without Thinking

The flowering quince opens
its red umbrella in a rain
that blurts out the story
of the earlier flowers:
the glitter of their pollen,
who they were, how they died
in a watered down light
among ferns afraid to look
using their fans at the
crucial moment
of disintegration.

Noise Puts It to Flight

Early morning dogs barking through gauze,
morning dead set against mountains moving
in place: I wake only to the bones,
my mind so constructed
I shall in the end be always at a toss,
migrating between losses:
one flounder's eye
passing through his body
got lodged in the thought
of wanting to emerge.
Like that. This dream of dogs
barking some sense into mountains.
There was a world. A mountain
lived on it all of its life.
There was a girl dancing in preparation
of life without a body. Eventually
I will tell all my bones how save
for a certain inconsequence
there was nothing in them
I wished to change.
How they mounted the snow
as if it were nothing!
And took to the hills
my gold eye
without looking back
for the uprising.

All the Activity There Is

Morning and raining,
raining and morning,
the first soft ashes
of light hit the boathouse
again and again:
all the muffled horns
on a faraway highway
blowing the dice of lights
like coals in your hands:
see, see,
see how sorrow can
derange a man's mind.

The Melancholiacs

How often our joy burns out
in November's hollow purple
where the fog's yellow lint
snags on the nail of a tree.
Our selves as well vanish
like a fanfare of sheep herded
over a covered country bridge;
it's another night of rain
in the hourglass
where the same thought
quietly inverts itself.
What to do with our
burnt-out joy?
Both before
and after, the farmer
spit something black
on the water, then
smiled,
his tobacco teeth
a load of monks
in the smallest of all
cathedrals.

The Compulsion to Adoration

The nudes are not far off . . .
and the lake waiting in the distance
where the blank birches cling
like a pool of milk between two hills
and the girls standing transfixed
eating their chocolate as if
it were candy. Tell the lake
not to open its glass eye
until this is the only moment
and they the only ones near.
A wink, a kiss: these are the
only signs. Beyond them, steeples
tower all the way to the sea
and the ship's compass
points to an iron hulk
drifting in the night.

Swimming Thinking Sleeping

Your arm stuck in the air
in the middle of a wave
like the dovetail joint of a drawer
somehow. Your legs pumping
and an organ sac moist and rolling
tucked in your gut
like a fat silver tick
where nerves nesting like spiders
are learning to crawl.
I tell you the lip-world is closing:
you could be saying good-bye
to eye-lust and life-pride
(it would be world-like)
though your tongue is invisible
and your hand the mere head
of a pin as you drop, noiseless
and catching on nothing and oh
the dusk of such speech at such times
bringing this to the already-
drowned!

Life on Earth Without Speaking

One season abandoned us
without leaving room for another.
Life on earth without speaking's
arrived. The courage of the rain
falling with a spear coming out of its mouth!
I'm out making space
as best I know how
but God's contradicting
even the plot in which
we are ruined: it's part
of the final vertigo.
Trees aren't able to endure.
Deer cry, lost in the soaking fog.
Soon we'll be mixed, blue ghosts
waltzing in search
of the theme.

II

How History Begins

On Avenue Brugmann indigo magpies
fly off the balconies.
A black iron railing keeps you
from falling into the absurd little
garden with its own iron fence
around flowers dozing over their own
graves. A few French children
sailing their boats in a sandbox,
one bright boy making a puddle
of piss for his own. You notice
in his hands there's an apple
stolen from lunch. His mother's
deciding what she would do
if he takes a few bites
and his penis drops off
withered somewhere.
And a cat who's been sunning
leaps perfectly down
for some small thing in the grass!
You've never seen such incurables:
leapfrog, leper, mother and child,
the sun strapped to his witness post,
you in your spot as the landscape
takes on a whole burning town
full of onlookers who cry
by god it shall not go down
when it does just that

and history begins
when someone arrives on the scene
to cover his face with his hands
like a clock.

The Voices

How many of you
would not have spoken at all!
Preparing myself for sleep
I'm startled by one of three small bones,
an extract from the inner ear
deeming itself so large
it begins to forge new sounds.
As if chance, getting to know me,
plucked his eyebrow once or twice
and intricate procedures
were set into motion
like jewels:
the body unwoven to an outline,
the root-ends of solitude
already sprouting into new voices
no longer dependent on being heard.
I hear them coming from the inside,
my whole night shifting like leaves
turning toward sun. They tell me
they are coming from the outside.
Think how your own
keep hearing their own:
into the same distance
a thousand sheep grazing on short grass
raise heads all at once
hearing something newborn awake
inside of themselves a hunger
to move on over the gas-white hills
in every extraordinary direction.

The Intended

One wants so many things . . .
One wants simply, said the lady,
to sit on the bank and throw stones
while another wishes he were standing
in the Victoria and Albert Museum
looking at Hiroshige's "Waterfall":
one would like to be able to paint
like that, and Hiroshige wishes
he could create himself out of the
Yoro sea spray in Mino province where
a girl under the Yoro waterfall wants
to die, not quite sure who her person is,
but that the water falls like a sheet of tin
and another day's thrown in the sieve:
one can barely see the cherry blossoms
pinned up in little buns like the white hair
of an old woman who was intended for this hour,
the hour intended to sit simply on the bank
at the end of a long life, throwing stones,
each one hitting the water with the *tick* of
a hairpin falling in front of a mirror.

True to Life Also

It's as though today
were found at the bottom of Escambia Bay
and an hour floated up in italics:
you can tell by the faces of those you love
tiny linguistic features
are beginning to appear on your own.
Yes, it's hot, almost evening,
and the children go screaming
over short green grass,
their heads fall apart
like great white peonies
and I have lain and almost
waited, wished for a flood:
the first star rising as a little bug
on the whiskey glass
while a wasp's nest rots in tomato light
with its seeds in a casket of gel.
The rasp of insects coming on
and going off like an oven
in which things grow tender.
Like an oven in which
I have lain, almost waited,
wished for a flood, while
the light filtered up from the sea
like filings to a magnet,
until salt grains dried
on the neck's edge.

Stamina

The man's trying to learn something new
every day. Yesterday and today he's been
in a demolished car eating peanuts straight
from a bag. Ahead are the remains of his
wife's house, out front the rusted navy of
his ingenuity salutes him: Kenmore, Waring,
Electrolux, hats off! From top and bottom
scrap metal he found a canteen that survived
a sequence of wars. He tried tuning his rosebush
once, a pink moth got caught ascending
in perfect pitch. He believes he'll keep
finding harmony in all things until the
day he dies. He's kept at it.
Now he can't stop admiring peanuts,
pops off their new jackets one by one
little naked bodies looking marvelous.
He marches them into his mouth.
His wife thinks he's crazy.
He circled everything she pointed at:
three steps of pink marble
lead to his brain's empty pool.
He's seen men on either side
pruning trees.
They stop work at noon and eat simple
lunches scooped out of their hats,
whole pears replaced in the space
perfect for stealing.

Lady Throwing Crackers to the Sea

Maybe she needs to be out there
with the mist like a spider
floating in space.
The saltines are dissolving
faster than aspirin
in a ravening stomach.
She took off her gloves.
She took off her socks.
Maybe she's getting the feel
of a statue.
Maybe she's coming to life.
I fed my doll Cream of Wheat
from a spoon and didn't think
anything of it.
Go to the last time
you didn't know what
you were doing.
A box of crackers is gone!
Like pages of your life
that didn't sink in,
you must have been thinking
of some other thing:
maybe she's getting revenge.

The Least Sequence of Flesh

Scum on the lake rim,
puffed fish
beating their heads against the shore
like beautiful albinos of love.
Cell tissues in an out-and-out whitening
that will drag on all day,
blueflies mating over the slick rot.
Clouds in their civilization
go no further, dissolving in rains.
Something lifeless provokes you
to throw yourself away entirely.
Think of the twin worlds
into which you have never wholly fallen!
You stammer and cling
to the edge of a cup
in the shape of the world.
The light almost undresses you,
eyes rinsing and rinsing
a strange and accurate detail
of what you think you see
like algae on small breasts
coming from water.

The Only Desirable Sequel

There's algae on small breasts
coming from water with a girl
unable, in her composure, to distinguish
friend from stranger.
There's a man unable to distinguish
what he is and what his wishes are
while he's waiting for what he sees
to happen to him, the way a master
takes hold of the model's half-length
and all things respond:
on the quaking gel of a pond
two white ibis
dissolve in a feathery light.
Like a child able to tell color
a girl picks the green from the white
while a man is mixing the two
with the devil's attention to detail:
something the eye loves to see,
an accident like pure birth
needing to be rinsed on the spot.
But the bather lies down
in an unrevealed future,
takes the sun total of days
on herself, and learns
how to dry.

Arrogance, Arrogance

Especially when there was no money
I would have gone mad
but I would go and have a look
at young Lorenzo: his terra cotta
head, those lips speaking to me
the way a rain rubs words
off the newspage.

after an adolescent by Donatello
and for Charlotte Novitz

The Singer's Face

Ach mein sin
         Wo willst du endlich hin?

How many ways of phrasing
there were in the old days!
Do you not remember
forming to yourself the singer's face
and mouthing all of the words?
One note was the perfect failure
to see yourself clearly.
The next, and your surroundings
completely changed.
Sing it now, who knows what
might happen? Music, like magic,
may work backwards; your senses
may be restored. Think
how the woods fill out
and the birds file in
when the eastern phoebe starts
with her sweet minor zest
on a branch where the buds
like vowels are about to be opened
by the bees who drone in the herbs.

Brute Notion

Why can't you go on like this, bare
and walking through the crosswinds
of a desert, nothing to eat and
no name?

Look what you've done with the
letters we've sent: flag-tissues balled
in the sweat of your hand.

Our children will grow up believing
in stories!

The rise and sway of time it
will take, to erase the dust
from the sand.

And they still might resort to the
single raspberry your brain has become,
or its mirage, a pyramid of red gems
rising before you at the scrabbled end.

Good King Wenceslaus

Word of mouth has it
you've been translated
into another gibberish
closer to your own.
Your friends rub their eyes
like a crossed-out passage
concerning what they *were*
most interested in.
All their thanks
like little salmon
are found dead halfway up
to your heart.
As for the family,
the holiday's just begun:
out back by the silver can
a single tinsel's shining
on the last trashed bough
of Christmas.
They're hoping it will come home
to you, fresh from its death
like the old divine.

White Risk

I can't see the difference between stars
shining with the quiver of an insect's
eye and your skin taking the light
wherever I watch myself touch you,
you who can't tell the difference
between your own true loves
sparkling with a thousand exceptions,
but I know
it makes a difference up there:
stars might give birth to a planet
spawning in the gap that spins out
a room for itself
the way our own room widens
as we awake in the same moment
to the same stars
with no way of knowing
if one is beginning to ease off,
loosening its warm hold,
or how soon it might be
before the gap closes in
like an infant's skull
soon after it senses being born
closes its doors, locking the world
inside. Mothers and fathers
keep counting your sons and daughters:
in many worlds
the species is endangered
that grows too great.

Albinism with Blue Irides

I have done nothing
for long periods of time
and learned to do it well.
If I fall silent, I am being continuous.
I am not overcome; do not be taken in.
The opal in my eye is a sedative.
Glimpsed once, an albino's death
cannot distinguish itself from
what lives. It is madness, to be
sure, but it happens. An albino
allowed to breathe in both worlds,
like an amphibian's love, exists,
as beauty without color exists
and breathlessness also is ours
now we are side by side
like an insight and error
occurring together:
look over our shoulders
how the lovers fall apart
like soft white rice
and do not grow old
on purpose.

In the Process of Elimination

Blue daylight: a little edge
provoked beyond measure. A man
standing at the windowsill
makes his decision between
having the house, the tree, or the car.
His eye's held to a landmark,
all things between them
ascending at once in a riot
of replica tints: the azure
and or of another light
somewhere smaller and deeper
and more toward the end
where he won't have the strength
to put himself in his own situation.
Outside there's a row of empty trees,
the backdrop for thirty years,
though he had hoped against each day
the way one leans on a tree
for shade in the clay afternoon.
And he's thinking of a house
without leaving, where a man
might lie down and not be startled
by the shifting of floors,
and driving all night on the highway
clean to the beach
where an ankle
is carved on the suds.
Certain areas he's left for a purpose,
like a little love provoked beyond

measure to the point of an imbecile
moving into his mind, its interminable
vegetable leafing and leafing,
absorbed with a luminous torture
like the cross section of an accident
into its own dark mass.

Almost As If To Tell Me

We read in the morning papers
how a passenger train broke up,
one car shoved in another
like a celestial telescope,
each death receding completely
from the center.
A life can't succeed so well.
With a casual horror
our little roses near the open butterdish
broke open, overlapping their own edges.
Perhaps one life in a thousand:
had it been yours
instead of mine
I do not know
what that would have
meant to me.
You pushed back your chair
with a set of bones
in which you have a faith
that has been pulverized.
And your voice,
an hourglass in which
the unknown is rapidly disintegrating,
had it been living or dead
it would have been useless.

Face: Rear View

Turning in September
the sourwood was left
to mature in our minds.
Imagine the being who
would do just that: her face
in the rearview mirror, frozen
by the first white shadbush
that April, broke off its statue
with a wince.

Lord, I don't know what
she saw, but someone has placed
the earliest signs in my mind,
where I can't help but see them,
and I am doomed to drive miles
of open road with the thought
of her mouth, and that cry
too late to be counted
among her only words.

Her Rival

Not much can exhume her:
not one glass of white brandy
taken in the middle of a blizzard
so dense it looks like nothing.
It's *mirabelle:* they say one ton
of pure plums is crushed
in the making. It may be untrue
but it's necessary
like the essential lie
that might save her.
She wants a slow death
like black ribbon
wound many times on
the dancer's instep
keeping volatile rags
stuffed in a toeshoe. The audience
twittering in red seats.
It seems inconceivable
anyone with the whole realm
of human activity to choose from
should hit on such a thing.
But it takes a magnificent dancer
or her rival
to sit through a storm
and feel finally freed
by an ache in her foot
to go wild with inhibition.

Reasons of His Own

I saw him paring his nails.
Later on comes the story:
first watch the green dust
of sunlight settle on
overgrown leaves in the meadow.
The like of which now happens
and my boy goes out walking
to the foot of the hill
with a knife in his pocket
that opens and shuts like a
snapdragon. I know what he does
out there. He cuts things up.
Whole pigeons, if he could find them.
He'd slice a moon on each wing
before letting them go,
liking the world best
when it leaps from a grave.
He comes home at night.
He washes his hands.
He can get them absolutely clean.
How can I tell him his heart
is a knife? That his mother's heart
holds the blade in a purse?
I suppose it can wait.
Like a killer in hiding
he'll think for himself
when the moment is right:

now on the meadow's edge
the rehearsal of insects
begins in their blood
like a native song.

Night String of Violin

Where the body lies there's the faint odor

of small flowers.

Violin string wound

round his throat

in the dark.

The bow is still missing.

A larger instrument is tucked

under the one-armed moon:

long and crescentic,

it's implicated

in the scattered chaff

of her past.

Is it enough to know

the woman went mad in her own arms,

when white and ivory trillium

appeared overnight

like footsteps in rapid pursuit?

Reader, Ride By

If I have led you into this solitude
by means of identical gesture
you shall stay only so long
as the length of leash it's taken.

Your memory will build rooms
for the imposition: if you've
one word left, save it for sudden
consolation, like a jigger of rye
held in the mouth for years.

There will be measurements other
than those you know. A bar of soap
washed down to its pith pinpoints
a new beginning. You will look forward
to the thrill, searching the house
for things about to disappear.

Without eating you'll take to
picking your teeth, every gesture
with a clarity as if for the last time
though whether they be your last gestures
or last clarities I'm uncertain:
that much is up to you.

When the fighter pilot drops a pamphlet
or balloon in your lap, grin and wave:

this means the end of your nights.
By morning the skywriting will pale.

Fantastic birds will be flowering in trees
where delicate bells are falling like fruit,
delight out of this world in which you will
wake like a master of rare knowledge in an
astonishing lapse of attention and hear
nothing, as if it had snowed all night.

The Tomb in Ghent

In the morning to see the cathedral!
It's filling with the yeast of a
rising light like the light-hole
of a grave briefly flooded before
the bodies come in. Charles is
buried somewhere in here:
Charles the Bold of Burgundy
(built like a barrel organ)
wanted a midget globe, and
something to do with his hands
like tossing an orange
to his daughter Mary, little
Mary of Burgundy in the corner crypt,
three feet away from her father.
She grew to be eighteen
and breasted with brass apples
on an effigy dress.
Mary likes to speak of her death.
Oh she says and then Oh
and again Oh, but every one hundred
days the word gets smaller from
young girls rubbing her lips
with their fingers asking her
what it is like. Oh she says
and the brass grows bright
like a halo over a secret:
Charles took a few to his grave.
He was killed while hunting
when a horseshoe hit his temple.

Now he covets the littleness
of his visitors who come
from all parts of the world
to touch his head like a lucky thing
and the brass grows bright
like the eyes of the charwoman
who bathes him with sponges
for a few extra francs.
She lights candles for him.
They throw shadows on the wall
like a pantomime of stallions.
All the little hoofprints
on Mary's bodice glow.
There was a moment like this
in their lives.
Oh said the king
and out ran her prayers
like a tiny troop of players:
back came an answer
and the light cried
let the old man in.

Old Lunes

Your habits are transfixed without you:
the way you look at the floor, it misses
you, it won't look up.
Smoke wreathes in an empty room, searching
for cigarettes you've taken away.
The dust on the window says *clean me*
in Greek. Your voice can't sleep, won't
speak, sits in the night table drawer
like a hen. Your favorite coat found
a note in its pocket: *life is strange.*
They keep doing the things you used to do.
Your clothes shake themselves out,
roll up their sleeves, spit on their gloves.
The toil of colognes trying to find you
in the garnished air!
Your whiskey's stopped eating, the wine's
run down to a blue rim.
Dishes arranged in a retrospective
on the drainboard. In the mirror
there's the sadness of a scapegoat's rival
who can't stop seeing himself
like this. He looks like a shipwrecked
saint. Idol of an island, his job is to wear
your silver ring with the missing intaglio
of a horse.

Tongues

There's a zealousness forming
in ancient rocks lodged on the arctic floor.
Stars on a fast for three thousand years
they're beginning to budge
like a tongue coming out for food.
They're talking about it in Brussels
with the flat faces of Flemish angels
about to burst over a lamb at Easter
like the roots of a paradise tree
making it through concrete in South Carolina,
cracking a path for the flood.
A tongue is an aim's length
and its aim is the next tongue
in a long line of tongues
each unable to tell where he stands
in the funnel. And the tongues of lovers
play a hand, exposing themselves
and passing it on
like a brief and unprintable poem.
There's something hidden under
your own tongue: it's hoarding a morsel
and passing it on in a universal maneuver
destined to work in time.
When the fisherman mending his nets
pulls apart a little fringe of shrimp
caught in his teeth
then spits on the water,
mark my oath on the chopping block:
I've seen the seahorses

wagging their tiny curls.
One will sink from the weight
of what's lashed on his back
and dash to the rockbottom
feeding the end of the line.

Twin Trees

And two permanent birds! Hand-sewn
baubles on a hairnet, just two:
others dropped off during the early years
when someone took hold of the acrobat's hair
and pulled him straight up to heaven, baring
his teeth: and his ankles took hold of his
brother's hands, praying there'd be some end
in sight: they flew together like a
decision, against their religion, to go
mad. They lost everything they had
but the birds. Their sequins fell
and turned into a tarnished lake.
So goes the saying when you look
at the trees on St. Godfrey's hill.
There's a world over their shoulders
and another on top of that
where a salamander on stilts
is hoisting his daughter into the arms
of her husband. Soon they'll have a child
to lift, whose head, in a year or two,
will break through the lake
into the amazement of his shadow
about the size of an oak leaf drifting
in October, when a few things fall
and fly with an ease through
the air he's learning to breathe.

The Heart of a Lieutenant

Open the flower:
a champagne bottle and a dancer
are living deep inside.
Now you must choose between them
as though this were the
beautiful room with no doors.

Let yourself go.
Like a stiletto, three times
to the hilt, retrace
the first entry
until there's some proof
this is real:

A woman in a larger woman's dress,
one straw hat moving by itself
through the thick of field glasses
and the world proposing to end
with a toast to the dead, rising
from trenches like a fountain of tulle
before the final vision goes flimsy:
row after row of faces like tiny buttons
difficult to undo in your mind.

The Wife of Mission Rock

Nothing curves at sea,
and the men there die abruptly,
in imitation of the fact, except
when the ship rises higher than necessary
and then they must drop suddenly
but for a long time,
so that their deaths appear natural
in the end, and the women sweeping the courtyards
pause, thinking the dust
to be the cause of a specific dryness
in the mouth. They leave half of a
pastry to harden on a plate.
They leave all of the lemons and figs
in bowls. They leave fuschia
splattered on the stone steps leading
down to the bay. They carry their brooms
with them, keep sweeping the air,
cleaning it back to the sea.
They sweep the sand from the shore,
feet standing in neat little rows of foam.
Each at the edge of something when
the foghorns remind them:
they will not clearly remember it,
they will not altogether forget it.
They will wait for something to emerge,
like a man at sea carving his children
from soap. One woman will start the rumor
that the sea is deeper than necessary:
Tell her, when has anyone ever come back
for one day's effort on earth?

Torture

It is not far
before the orchards blow out,
a blue-yellow blindness
in all of the fields.

Pale evening dun
on the river. Blouses
will open
under the buckeye,
the husk of your speech
fall off in the cold blue night,
and the idea of anything *modern*
escape you.

As Many As Nine

From under a hunter's moon
yellow leaves fall in the black night,
fatting the land.
How many single travelers
traveling on a single night,
a nameless yeast in their blood!
I met a man leaving our village
which he mistook for another.
Friend, he said, you cannot understand
these places unless you have never
been there.
His hand on the hill
in the open air, almost a star,
struck me as the ideal torment.
Though knowing how to go on
might get him there in good time,
these rumors of a pig's feast
seep into my bones like oil:
the hunters enter the woods
the woods enter our lives
think of the deer in us
the tiny horses of Troy there are
in a world congested
like a baby born with eight or nine hearts
on a planet with as many moons.

Nameless the Space

Not where she was met but left,
like a lover of water standing in a
wood, she would walk sometimes.
Her house a light far away, not yet
lit, confided in her with the difficulty
of two things used to being one inside
of the other. And then a crow.
From a few black spots on the
rich and yellowing wings of a monarch
he burst, a full-grown bird
out of an acre of pumpkin.
His amazing lower lip still quivered:
The world's sewn shut!
All living gut and gill and breath-sac
deflate in deep night.
Withdraw from the moonlight!
Then he was gone, raising
an eyebrow out of his body.
God in his lifetime
will live to live in another.
As she will walk this way again,
the shiny curds of his dead face
heaped under the nut-brown moon.

The Inspector of Miracles

It depends on how you gaze at it:
this little incomparable,
as unpredictable as a bee
in the hotel jam
taken at once for what it *was*
as though you were certain the dead
started living again after setting foot
in their heart's desire.
You are not here to expect
miracles. But it serves
as a charming introduction
to the inspector himself
who's just now on an endless round.
Consider the host of other things!
A little basket full of loaves
warm and rising like blisters.
Butter in a cobalt tub
lazy and gold, rich in oils.
Cut lemon and cubed sugar,
two pots, cream that pours
slowly and stays on your lips
leaving one red napkin
with a luminous ring.
Consider your own setting foot
in the heart's desire:
you might not be this happy again.
Look at it this way,
as if it were real,
as if you were singing to the household saint

who grew tired of waiting and sang to himself
till the whole house was certain
and singing again.

Gigantic Brazen Head

> To think deeply right now
> would terrify me.
>
> —E. S. Connell

4–1   All day singing the plum-tree tune!
Watching the florist and wanting to be
the ringmaker's orchid, pinned to her
breast by the shoemaker's hand, a master
of the female half-length, imagine!

4–2   If there are other lives
(never an insect, lord)
let me be five-thirty light
on the wall: a confectioner's
bride trying to pinpoint her
threshold, lambent and thrilling
down to my slipper.

4–4   I once was the perfect square
of my own blue tile, and
later became *that* blue.
But you couldn't confine me:
all of my memories I put
out to pasture.

4–6   Bluespike nearer the house,
Snakeroot in the garden,
Bergamot by the lake.
Bluebells last a long time on
the stem, and grow in clumps.

A bee on my lips!
My decisions I'm certain will
always be excellent:
I merely question my ability
to carry them out.

4–9 And at some time, please: a plum.
The luxe of it! But let it be blue
like a grape. What was it before?
The child of a priest, perhaps.
Falling from grace like an art.

4–12 *Never* a little sardine tin lying
open at noon near a hot window.

4–16 Little by little a latent image
is beginning to appear as the
cardboard or canvas it was.

4–17 A terrible clawing in me.
It's the day past,
trying to tell me
it is not half so worthless
as I had imagined.
Consider my astonishment
without it!

4–20 Woebegone.
if only I were *free*
to be a tugboat.

Woebegone, the word,
if I were *only* the word—

4–22   All day listening to a radio sermon
with the life span of a sea slug:
things need not even exist to affect us.

4–26   Caged in the late rain
at the harbor.
Oh hope: downfall,
blue dun on the bay tide.
There are no tolerable dimensions.
But I'm reduced to them.

4–28   I can't help lingering,
but there's no reason why
anyone should know I'm still here.

5–10   Dew season now:
large and solitary flowers grow
wherever they think unfit.

The Simplest Possible Arrangement of an Iris

Once, twice, three times
blue:
fields flowering in purple.
All over Greece
white rocks roll out of the jars
and down hills
in the simplest possible
arrangement:
a wild tribe
breasted with cowrie shells
standing in the field
like iris!

III

Persistence Beyond Recognition

You think you have noticed the process
of lighting, the particular way in which
it takes place: but at half past five
lighting becomes reading, the room
darkening with vowels until you are
forced to begin again, out loud.

Stems in one hand, scissors in the other,
suddenly you are arranging the things you
say, hear, read, in an order from darkest
to lightest, and cannot name the roses
emblazoned with color so strong, each one
seems married to a different word.

You are led very quickly into another
world, the first forms of words undressing
before you. Already you are under the
impression you'll need two lives:
one's a picture in your mind the other
is busy preparing.

Putting your books side by side on
the shelf, together in their right
order, it occurs to you this is not
their final place. Light's only now
reaching the point where you have
something to say:

Candle of the third vowel! Light

on the page, light on the wall,
of your eye and in the margin,
descending into a handful of roses:
red deepening to most red, reddening
to the very reddest.

Evening exists. It comes always.

Where There Is Such a Thing

Being in that dank and rotten
cellar room was beautiful,
where whole heaps
of indistinguishable objects
go pale, breaking into the sweat
of being looked at by moisture,
and little is lonely if seen
by itself: onions, ten times more
brilliant than natural dew, and
potatoes, with a third, fourth and
fifth eye, praying to be kept on
like tenants afraid of disassembling
in their own skins. While
the rat, gleaming with reverie,
realizes each success is a repetition
of the moment he made up his mind.
Despising things of interest
he takes an interest in himself,
where there is such a thing as being
shut in, and though his tunnel
lets in the sound
of being out on the streets,
the dead down here are happy:
though they never actually lived
there was always that hope
in being barely able to hum.

Little by Little

Gangplank on the horizon:
I have come eleven or twelve miles
in three and one-half hours
depending on nothing
but weather, clouds
jibbing early out.
Though I am not at sea
I have that feeling:
a better chance of surviving
in less space.
For two days I've followed
a flat bracelet of ducks
until they turned
into jet vapor, an olive streak
I followed until I was spineless
and sick, with nothing left
to spill from my sack.
Why part of me has yet to begin I can explain:
identical camels in a great crossing
will often start out
one hundred days apart.
And today
I saw salmonberries
shrink back to their branches!
Even the upright ash
of a sumac won't fall,
or an ear of corn in shock
listening to winter.
I call out to my beginnings

stay where you are
your hurry has already wasted in me.
Lower and lower
a long rope comes
from out of the sky.
While the asparagus,
asserting itself,
pushes its tip
through the loam.

Arson

My face lives by itself

in a small separate cave

with a candle in each eye

lit by a cruel remark:

Lord, I thought I was the only one,

but I see hundreds of them:

Each one is traveling

toward the wrong country,

each one's face shines

like the mouth of a thief

who has stolen the last fat sheep,

eating it under the moon.

Tell Her

A lake pink with mud
a lady with milk leg is
wading to bring me an
idea:
                    perfect

that her walk comes
to this point, a spoon
standing in thick soup.

When will she cross
my field full of tiny
streaked flowers, skewering
them on her leg's
thin spindle?

A black pistil pops
inside the sensitive tulip.

Think damn it
on the brink of your death
I want you to think.

An Examination of Suffering

Could be cuspids dangling
on gum-scrap: two icicles
outside my window hang on
what looks like sheer will:
half of me waits with a quiet
tension for the sound of what
happens next: the other half
waiting on a fragment completely
finished with two loose ends:
while the wind, it's clear,
wants them both.

Men in Trees

Start at the top:
an orb weaver moaning
from silk in her glands.
Slide down.
Tree frogs stacked on the
wet tree's tendon.
Lower by an eye
the slip-elm's nippled
with mushrooms.
This could be it:
Stop sawing,
do limb work,
close in on what
you are doing
without touching ground:
it could kill you,
like an ordinary man.

Life Is Blameless

March fell out of the pie
like a blackbird.

All my alternatives
whisked off the lawn
by his bright orange beak.

Now I'm lonely,
which is death.
And death is lonely
for my own true self.
Now my own true self
slips under the limbo stick
one more time.

Soon the poppyheads
will go limp
as the guillotined.

Poetry Breeds an Animal that Can Promise

The coon on two paws
in a hazel crotch:
his point-blank eyes
suddenly give leaf
to wonder!
He's high on something
he's scrounged,
this or that scrap
makes him feel clean,
clear of his former details:
his feeling of thiefness disappears
making a little promise
it won't happen again
in exchange for the core it took
to get this innerness
that keeps on rinsing
his surroundings away
till only his eyes are left,
rimmed with the pity he's beginning
to feel at this tantalizing moment
when life's never been so unfair
or more at a showdown:
there, to the left of the hazel leaf
he's beginning to brook in the sky!

I Sicken for Sweetness of the Heart

To be precise I can be likened
to nothing today but my longing
for a little likeness at all.
I've eaten only one hard egg
a lemon and white salt
on my pillowcase
next to the lake.
Dare I swim?
The water's a bloodbath
from a week's worth of rain.
There's a sibyl on the springboard.
The lovers of poetry wander
in a region on the far shore
and they kiss,
grafting their throats together
like fruit trees.
From them no world.
Their fruits ripen on my hands.
God, look here,
these are my enemies
whom I wish to protect
and covet.
Though the temptations
of an anchoress
are more than a few,
two blueberries
lodged in the eyes
of a dove
will suffice.

The House of His Own Undoing

Spare me
the novelty
of having to think:
your flower-skirt
synchronized to fall
and inflate
won't work
in deep water:
and spare me
your fish
whose flesh falls apart
in the same white pleats.
I'll take nothing
to do: let the jonquil
fume in my rosé bottle
over the oval seal of
a Portuguese plaza
where a harlot
will tap me on the shoulder
later tonight
and I'll fall apart
dancing
under the first yellow star.

An Apology for Not Saving the Children

I was the man in the boat
wanting to smile at you.
I wasn't trying to expose myself.
I was waiting for the right thing
to say, one line grown to rope
thick enough to haul up my anchor
and show you, it's smiling.
I wanted to reach you before
the storm got in your way,
before nothing could save you,
long before the water spun your statues
into the dead and left them there
like a pile of drying oars.
Believe me now, if you can.
I was trying to tell you
there is no reason to be afraid:
even when a grown man wakes
from his dreams breathless and uncertain
he's only imagined the thunder
banging like a child's piano over the lake
and the children running in every direction
bright as pickup sticks
in their wet clothes.

Before an Enormous Building

My back aches, as though
I've been sleeping in a field
hidden by sleek wheat spires,
letting them carry a tall man's message
across countries to a dark girl,
bowing with perfect practice
before a hibiscus
she wants in her hair.
Perhaps I've been drunk for so long
I'll never know what's sufficient:
What does she want
and why am I here
lingering before an enormous building
with the bright red flower of my shame
and my back aching
as though I had built this
when there are so many lakes ,
in my life, I've done nothing
but float on them all.

Five Looks of the Infant Jesus

after Messiaen

Break me in pieces
with words if I'm wrong:
he's odd beyond
sympathy.

Look how he sleeps
through the livelong day
while something rattles
in the fig of his little fist
and keeps us from sleeping
at all!

This is not the way
hunger is supposed to appear,
yet how happy his mother looks
when the spigot of his mouth
determines the pose of her breast.

His whole body
oiled and curved
for the bath
looks like an eyeball
about to be placed
in its setting.

In the square
at this moment
the eyes of a bird

are put out: I
can't look at all.
And the baby starts
singing to himself!

At Cana

One by one we awoke
out of wine, an ordinary
absence we were prepared
to live through
when he took from his hand
a glass
something like the truth:
it appeared to be empty
when he took from his eyes
a thin film of oil
and anointed the rim continuously
until we heard music
filling air like fragrance
of sweet wine.
Then he took the still-beating
heart of a life that had been
recently joined and broke it
into syllables.
And our cups were filled.
Afraid to speak, we drank
until we were thirsty again.
We were given another set of
tears: even then,
we were not aware
our lives were becoming
a parable, alive:
we loved best how he failed
to show how it might be done
in the future.

Patient Without an Acre

Look how appropriately incomplete
I am: I never carry a pocket mirror.
My skin takes the light.
I don't know where it goes.
Maybe it passes right through me.
Maybe it follows me,
making me easy to follow,
for there's no mistaking
what it is: a life all right,
and my own, but to what end?
I can't work, much less love.
Love, there's no mistaking the word
for it: once you've driven the
wild breath in, you'll have
a little glass hammer,
perfectly useless. This,
the flint of all things!
They say one off another
we light our way with
what's been lit for us.
While my own dark risk
is not to grow, not
until I've given myself to a leper,
until he's touched my soul with his body
and together we work like the missing part
of a crossword.
Work, of which I wasn't able!
Love and work. *Lieben, Arbeiten.*
The little glass hammer is ringing!

There's another word for work
another word for love
a language with one word for both
and a country with no words at all.
Look at the men and women
unable to understand:
there are two of them walking
alone and in love
coming back from the fields
that have bent them.

Who Shall Have This

Who shall have this
laughter to himself?
It happens so rarely
and perfectly: already
in high, cloudy places
it's beginning to parcel
rewards: its moving trumpet-
call causes an ambiguity
to save someone's life.
From a distance it's love
and no wonder:
an angel is glimpsed/sliced
falling from heaven
straight through the wires
of her harp, her card-face
spinning on the spokes
of a bike's rear wheel
moving the air with
a beautiful clatter.